365 DAYS
OF EXTREME
MOTIVATION

THE ABILITY
TO SOLVE
PROBLEMS

INDEX

365 DAYS OF EXTREME MOTIVATION

BOOK 1

365 DAYS OF EXTREME MOTIVATION-

Chapter 1: Introduction

Living our daily lives can be as easy as taking a breath of air or as difficult as climbing a mountain peak.

There are things that can get us down and up. Even our own family can fill us with anger or enlighten us with joy and happiness. No matter how tall you are in life, you will always need someone, something, or anything to help you get through each day. Some people find relief in God, family, companions, dreams and ambitions.

To live a fruitful life is to live it with meaning. Finding that meaning can be a lifelong journey, and along the way you may need words of wisdom to guide you along the right path. Words that will allow you to overcome the struggles that come with what life has to offer.

Life is always unfair. Some are rich while others desperately seek ways to last the day.

If you are lucky enough to be given the destiny of a wonderful life, be grateful for it. If in any case fate has extended a cruel hand to you, do not hesitate. Life is a mixture of things. One that is full of many surprises.

Today may be hard, but tomorrow remains a mystery until you do something today to change what lies ahead. Make each day worthwhile for the next.

This book will give you some of the most inspiring advice that will help motivate you every day of the year.

Chapter 2: Motivational Listening Tips

1. "Wisdom is the ultimate reward you get for a lifetime of listening rather than being the one who speaks the words" - Sometimes it is better to keep your mouth shut and your ears open. The great and wise learned to listen before they became what they are.

2. "Listening is a great way to show respect" - Instead of being undisciplined, listening perfectly portrays the most sincere respect.

3. "Making a habit of listening will do you more good than words" - It is when people listen that they really become wise.

4. "People who probably have many friends and companions are the ones who excel at listening" - If you listen often to what people have on their minds, you are likely to win them over as your lifelong friends.

5. "Success can be earned by talking, but listening offers so much more, excellence" - Great individuals are formed and perfected by the ability to listen to others.

6. "Listening can allow us to be formed into much better individuals" - No leader in human history has not listened to someone in his or her life.

7. "The best literatures in the world were born from the language and the language of listening" - Even Shakespeare had to spend

some time soaking up the ideas of the individuals around him.

8. "Relationships are held firm through the storm not by talking but by listening" - Successful and fruitful relationships are produced by the power of listening to each other.

9. "The key element of good communication is the ability to listen to what is not being said" - There are times when listening requires more than our sense of hearing.

10. "When people speak words, keep each word in mind. Not everyone was given the gift of listening" - To be among those who stand out in a crowd of deaf people. Hearing words that no one else wants to hear.

11. "When you listen, do it for the sake of understanding and not just to build a response" - Conflicts are fuelled when people only listen to explode their emotions rather than to seek wisdom.

12. "True friends listen while false friends care less about paying attention" - If your friends are real, they will not hesitate to listen to you.

13. "Good conversations often come from good listening" - no matter how intimate a conversation is, it will never end well if you don't listen to each other.

14. "Doing anything else while listening is not

listening at all" - people can only do so much but not listen enthusiastically while at the same time doing something.

15. "The reason we were given a pair of ears and a single language is so that we could hear more than we can speak" - it may sound like an irrational way to defend talking too much about listening, but it definitely gives us the big picture.

Chapter 3: Conversations and Storytelling

16.   "Humans bridge worlds through communication and storytelling" - if you want to communicate better with someone or a good number of people, tell them a story they will never forget.

17. "Very often, people who tell great stories also end up with wonderful stories" - if a man preaches good things, great and unimaginable things will happen to him.

18. "The future holds great things for poets" - this is not literally poetry, but people who are great communicators become future leaders.

19. "The human race learns by thinking in images and capturing those images through stories" - whether you are a teacher or simply want to make your mark on people, the best way to do that is through communication with stories.

20. "The reality we live in can be very complicated. The best way to simplify it is in the form of stories" - this goes especially for those people who have children. The greatest concepts of life can be simplified simply by telling someone a story that is much easier for the mind to digest.

21. "Having stories in mind leaves memories for a lifetime. Sharing those stories makes them last forever" - if you want your stories to be remembered beyond your lifetime, tell them and share them with everyone.

22. "If you are telling a story, choose a big one or don't tell it. " - The stories we tell bring meaning and inspiration to those around us. Tell everyone a great story instead of something no one wants to miss.

23. "Stories unravel meaning without creating the mistake of defining it yourself" - there are cases where people have different points of view for each opinion but storytelling says otherwise. It makes sense without creating uncertainty and doubt.

24. "The world has long been shaped by the stories of our ancestors. Those stories are the reasons we exist in this world today" - aspiring leaders can change anything in this world but first, those individuals must be willing to risk themselves and their stories completely.

25. "An American Indian proverb once said: Those who tell stories rule the world" - it is true. Individuals who express themselves through stories become leaders and great people in history.

26. "There is nothing that hurts like keeping a story inside your head" - leaving a legacy doesn't have to be all action. It must also be through the stories you have shared all your life. There is no greater relief to tell your stories than to keep them in your grave.

27. "Stories lead people into an unknown world and into things that are not heard" - storytelling not only conveys your thoughts, but also awakens the interest of many and leads to a creative and innovative generation.

Chapter 4: Living a Life of Truthfulness and Transparency

28. "There is no true enlightenment in life if there is no transparency and truthfulness" - then and only then can we achieve peace and harmony throughout our lives if we choose to be truthful.

29. "We have to be honest with ourselves and say "NO" to those people and things that don't do us any good. The key to rediscovering yourself is to live honestly" - there are those who fall prey to those who oppress and tell lies. Free yourself from these chains that bind you by living your life with

truth and sincerity.

30. "There is nothing more valuable than a truth spoken and done. Telling the truth and living with it is a lifelong reward.

31. "Success comes into play when accountability, transparency, self-definition and truthfulness are fused as one" - there is more to success than meets the eye. It is not for the faint of heart and especially not for those who do not want to change their habits.

32. "Great leaders achieve greatness by passion and truthfulness" - it is not about the race you are, but about how truthful you can become. Leaders are elevated and exalted by their selfless passion and truthfulness.

33. "People tend to tear down their walls and show who they really are and what situation they are in, especially in desperate times.

34. "Be the person you really are and not a copy of someone else" - sometimes people are too influenced by others to become what they are supposed to be. Believing in you and being true to that belief makes anyone a better person.

35. "Be genuine, be authentic and not just a person that others would want you to be" - don't be ashamed to become who you really are. People will accept the truth once they start seeing it in you.

36. "There are those who trample on your existence but do not hesitate. Instead, become the brightest star and outshine everyone" - when people persecute you, it is often because they are afraid of what you might become. Continue to be who you are and later you will be more than anyone else.

37. "Be yourself because it's beautiful. Why would you stop showing yourself and create a facade to hide your true self?" - Life is beautiful and so are you. There's no reason not to let the world know who you are.

38. "Your true self is not represented by how others see you, but by how you show it to others" - the truth is that people will continue to believe what they see and what you do, make sure you mean your true self.

39. "Truth can never be kept hidden. It is like smoke rising in the air that does not go unnoticed" - never tell a lie or live with a lie. The truth will always happen anyway.

40. "Authenticity has a price of integrity, transparency and vulnerability" - these are the factors that make something or someone genuine.

41. "Being ourselves is more of a gamble. There is a risk of persecution and there is a risk of winning big" - truth always has a price. It is never easy, the stakes are high but the rewards are even greater.

42. "Hiding the truth in exchange for security

is not the best way to live" - in desperate times, truth demands to be sealed but doing so has a high lifetime price.

43. "With the truth within you, it is easy to become a better person than anyone else" - there is no shame in admitting the truth. No matter how difficult it is, the truth is always the best choice you can make.

44. "A transparent heart and a sincere life have no persuasive equal" - the driving force of influence is easily achieved by living your life without restrictive walls.

45. "The combination of kindness, honesty, transparency and humor works harmoniously for the common good" - no matter how large or small a group, key

factors will always be required to keep it strong.

46. "The absence of transparency creates the wall of mistrust and the confinement of insecurity" - the actions we take and the decisions we make create a ripple effect.

47. "When things and people are transparent, they are likely to be free of judgment and constraint" - people are less likely to think negatively about something that is purely positive.

48. "Transparency makes the soul easier to see" - when we truly live with transparency, no one can judge us, ever.

49. "Transparency is seen both physically and mentally" - transparency coincides with the way we do things and how we think about them.

50. "The life we live should be as transparent as the freedom we have" - it is quite clear what freedom is to us. Now, it is who in turn needs to be transparent.

51. "The truth never harms a transparent and just cause" - when we see the truth, it immediately unfolds without a trace of doubt.

52. Never mistake transparency for love" - love is a beautiful thing and so is transparency. What your soul shows in transparency may not be the content of your

heart out of love.

53. The peace we so long for is also transparency for all mankind" - it is when we have reached a transparency that we can have peace.

54. "Democracy is the transparency that is portrayed" - like peace, transparency brings the freedom of democracy.

55. "For everything to work, accountability and transparency must be present" - the truth is that, for people to truly live in harmony, they must first be accountable and transparent.

56. "Wisdom speaks of many things, and

honesty is one of them" - the wise do not indulge in lies but embrace the truth.

Chapter 5: Cooperation and Teamwork

57. What makes society and our civilization work is the collaboration of individual commitment.

58. To be champions, people must work together to become an unbeatable team.

59. Teamwork fuels the achievement of a common vision.

60. Alone, one can achieve much, but together greatness is next in line.

61. Then and only then can a team work as one when they have established trust.

62. Personal ambition must not override teamwork, otherwise it will not exist.

63. As they always say, two heads are better than one!

64. The principle is to unite as one. Keeping the team intact is progress and working as one is already a success.

65. Success won't be ahead if you work as a team, but it will continue constantly.

66. The pillars of a team are each member and each individual is the team.

67. Collective intelligence is always worth more than just a glimmer.

68. To make fire, you need two stones and not just one.

69. Unity is the strength that a team has and that a single person can never have.

70. Teamwork is based on altruism. The more you have less consideration for yourself, the stronger the team becomes.

71. A team with one goal is unity and success

combined.

Chapter 6: The Beauty of an Open Mind

72. Keeping your eyes and ears open is also about being open to learning and wisdom.

73. To seek something is to seek to achieve your goal. To find something on the other hand is to discover what is unknown.

74. An open mind cannot be withheld from education and knowledge.

75. Open your mind with feedback on your actions, whether good or bad.

76. There is no such thing as negative criticism of an open mind.

77. To persuade people you must have an open mind and listen to them first.

78. Trust is not about having all the answers to every question, but about being open to every question to be answered.

79. A fraction of your life is what happens naturally, and the rest is how you react to it.

80. A pessimist usually complains about everything; an optimist anticipates change; while open-minded realists adapt to circumstances.

81. Clear your mind before entering into a conversation. A cloudy mind does not work well.

82. The most difficult thing is to decide to act; the rest depends basically on the perseverance of an open mind.

83. In every day, either you lead the game or the game leads you.

Chapter 7: Versatility

84. In life, winning is not the years of profit but how you adapted to the circumstances that made you a winner.

85. The strongest and the smartest do not necessarily mean the ones that last. Sometimes it takes more than that and something called adaptability.

86. If you are faced with several challenges, the only thing that can hold you back is the inability to accept change.

87. Life, in its own way, comes with changes

that we must accept. Those who do not accept change are those who fall behind in life's race.

88. Every successful organization is made up of people who are able to adapt to change.

89. Most individuals see opportunity as an exceptional occasion. Versatile individuals, on the other hand, see change as the spark of new opportunities.

90. The circumstances you have to endure in life can be redirected as favorable events if you have the ability to adapt.

91. Cold hard steel is useful until it is formed into something. Although it is a hard process,

the rewards are truly amazing. The same concept applies to changes in our lives. Although it is hard, it can be done and the results are worth all the pain.

92. Like water in a container, a wise person adapts to the circumstances around him.

93. When you let go of what you are, you will open the doors to what you could be most.

94. Life has many mountains to climb. Do not hesitate if you fall, for the journey in life is the reward for your difficulties.

Chapter 8: Fiery Passion

95. The passion within you feeds the dreamer who can change the whole world.

96. Living one life less than you could have achieved means that there is no passion in your life.

97. Growth, knowledge and wisdom never end for those who have the passion to keep learning.

98. Passion is the driving force that made the human race the supreme beings on this planet.

99. When passion drives you, let your reason guide you and you will go as far as your eyes can behold.

100. Before we can feel the passion within us, we must act it out to have an understanding of what it is.

101. To experience passion for someone who has never felt it before is like teaching light to a blind man.

102. The great leaders in the history of man have always had a passion within them to excel among others for the common good.

103. One good thing about passion is that it

cannot be faked.

104. A passionate beginning always ends with surprising results.

105. If you ask our leaders, they will always have a good story about how their journey was passionate.

106. Stop wishing for something to happen. If you really want something, turn that desire into passion and get what you want.

107. Love what you do. With love, you will do your work passionately and everyone else will follow.

108. Passion in life only runs out when we run out of breath.

109. It is worth waiting for people who have the same burning passion as you to settle for individuals who are unenthusiastic.

110. When we have passion, therefore, we can achieve.

Chapter 9: Delight, Surprise, and Happiness

111. If you decide to surprise your partner once in a while, you will realize that you will be surprised every time, too.

112. Don't tell people how you plan to do it, but simply tell them what to do and you will be surprised by the results.

113. Life is full of surprises and every day you will receive one or even more.

114. You may find that the truth is very rarely told to be so delicious.

115. Surprising others can be done simply, but surprising yourself is a totally different story.

116. Live each day with a surprise in mind. Expecting something every day gives you something to look forward to.

117. Problems between partners, love and war, can be overcome by surprise.

118. People like to stay within their comfort zones. The best way to bring about change is to surprise them.

Chapter 10: Simplicity

119. Simplicity is the best form of sophistication.

120. Goodness, truth and simplicity are united as one to achieve greatness.

121. A life lived in simplicity is not a life not lived well.

122. With simplicity comes ease, joy, and peace.

123. A simple work of art can tell as many

fascinating stories as a sophisticated work of art.

124. Don't complicate things when simple can do the job.

125. In this ever-changing world, sometimes the most difficult thing to find is simplicity.

126. Simplicity is majestic and can even surpass great sophistication.

127. The aim is not simplicity. It is the way to handle complicated things in a harmonious manner.

128. Simplicity is the catalyst for the

evolution of human life.

129. If you cannot explain something to a 5-year-old child, chances are you will not understand it either.

130. There is really not much in life that we do not know. It is only we who create the complications.

131. In any design, simplicity is about eliminating the obvious and leaving behind what is significant.

132. Free yourself from the entanglement of life. It is truly an easy journey waiting to be enjoyed.

133. Nature is sophisticated but in a very simple way.

134. Nature's simplicity tells us that the little things in life matter and that those little things make up everything.

Chapter 11: Gratitude

135. Be grateful for what you have and what you do not have. All men have had misfortunes but not all have had blessings.

136. Gratitude can be seen when one wants to give back the same amount for which one has been grateful.

137. The mere fact of breathing is a premise of life. As long as thou art alive, give thanks for it.

138. Be grateful for what you have been given until it is still there. Most of the time people

do not measure courage until they are left with nothing.

139. Blessings come to those who are grateful for what is given to them, whether great or small.

140. In every day of your life, give thanks. It is never written what comes after.

141. Be not angry if the roses have thorns, but be thankful that the thorn bushes bloom into roses.

142. Do not waste what you have now for what you do not have. Keep in mind that what you have now is only one of the many things you wanted.

143. Make a habit of being grateful for everything you have, big or small.

144. Let your gratitude be heard, and the blessings will overflow.

145. When thou art happy, give thanks. It is one of those moments in life that make life worth living.

146. Gratitude is not done simply by uttering words, but by living according to them.

147. Gratitude is a virtue.

148. People who are capable of being grateful

are also capable of achieving greatness in life.

Chapter 12: Goodness

149. Goodness is the only feature that distinguishes us humans from other creatures on this planet.

150. Goodness can be expressed simply by a warm and honest smile.

151. The goodness you sow will be the same goodness you will reap.

152. Reward kindness with the same amount given and it will never run out for the rest of your life.

153. Where there are people, there is a chance to spread goodness.

154. There should be no barriers or exclusions to goodness.

155. Be kind to everyone you meet. You may never know that they are fighting a harder battle than you.

156. Goodness is a language that any blind man can see and any deaf man can hear.

157. The mere act of kindness is worth ten times the intention.

158. A mistake in goodness is far better than

a good act with cruel intentions.

159. Be not ashamed to say kind words.

160. The act of kindness is reason enough to persuade others to be kind as well.

161. There is no greater act than that of kindness.

162. All the religions of the world teach kindness because it is a virtue.

163. All that you spend will be lost, and all that you keep will end up in the hands of others. But what you give to others will be something you can keep forever.

Chapter 13: Humility and Reservation

164. We are all equally human. You should never despise anyone unless you are lending a hand to help them up.

165. Humility is not to degrade oneself, but to avoid being self-centred.

166. Futile pride only provokes war, but humility initiates the revolution for peace.

167. For men of great power, humility is the most difficult thing.

168. Humility should not be something of which one is proud; otherwise, one would not have learned it in everything.

169. The act of humility is sometimes the most difficult thing to conjure up when one is in a moment of anger and despair.

170. The quickest way to earn respect is to learn humility and practice it sincerely.

171. Humility is that heavenly virtue of which not everyone has been blessed.

172. Swallowing pride is the first step in learning humility.

173. Humble yourself among others. Pride is but a useless but dangerous thing that can drag you down.

174. The proud person is always tied with his chain of commitment while the humble person is free of any restrictions.

175. Even if you have an enormous amount of talent, be humble because it is the right thing to do.

Chapter 14: The Act of Giving

176. Give and keep giving. No one has become poor simply by giving.

177. The act of unselfish giving is always rewarded with abundant blessings.

178. There is no limit to what we can give as long as we have the will to do so.

179. When you strive to give to others, you also give to yourself by investing in good deeds which you will later reap with blessings.

180. Giving is the willingness to let others experience the blessed life you have.

181. Create waves of goodness by initiating the act of self-giving.

182. Do not wait for others to lead you to become a generous, forgiving, compassionate and loving person. You can do it yourself and help others do it too.

183. You will lose everything you have bought. Others will take what you have saved but the things you have given to others unconditionally will give you something you can keep forever.

184. The more you give to others, the more

thanks you receive from this world.

185. There will be times when you will feel doubtful. Resolve those doubts by beginning to give to others.

186. Be content with what you have and share all that you can give to others.

187. The feeling you get from giving to others is like a life energizer.

188. Each day is a blessing. Use this opportunity not only to make yourself smile but also to make others happy.

Chapter 15: Persistence is Omnipotent

189. Being intelligent and talented on your own is often not rewarded. You need to be persistent to achieve the things you would like to have. You need to remember that talent is supreme and nothing can replace it.

190. As you pursue your goals in life, you need to have a persistent attitude and a level of energy that is purposeful.

191. Your continued personal growth is based on your persistence in achieving it. You never know when you will fully flourish as an individual. You have your own time

and with persistence, you will have a greater opportunity to reach your full potential.

192. Success does not happen overnight. You need to be driven and persistent. Without these two, you can never expect to find yourself on the road to success.

193. If you are already a persistent and resourceful person, you also need to make sure that these two traits do not make you an ignorant and stubborn person.

194. If you want to succeed in life, you must maintain a good level of enthusiasm, even after you have failed.

195. When you are faced with a difficult

situation, you should never avoid it but face it head-on.

196. When you try to make your point, being subtle and clever will not work. You have to make sure you get to the point. If it doesn't work the first time, do it again and again.

197. Be patient like a tree that grows enormously over time. Be persistent like the persistent growth of grass, even with consistent trimming.

198. Doing consistent things to achieve a goal defines your character, especially when you have done it constantly for three times or more just to get what you want.

199. When you live your life, you should maintain persistence like a small fire that burns within you. This will help you to get ahead as you go along.

200. Life is never easy and that is why you have to keep going no matter how difficult it is. This is the only way to clear your path and move towards a happy and fulfilled life.

201. If you want to always be at the top of your game and be the best at what you do, then you have to act like you are the last person on the line. In this way, you will always do your best and strive to be better.

202. We all have problems. If you want to get through everything you're going through right now, you have to make sure you keep

going and you have to keep holding on.

Chapter 16: Get Inspired Every Day

203. When you feel depressed, when you feel like you're about to give up, look around and appreciate the things you have. Find something to hold on to. Find something or someone to help you move on.

204. When you fall asleep, you will find yourself wondering about the things you did or the things you want to do. Discover your deepest desire that you believe will help you become a better person.

205. Simply asking yourself who you really are is not enough. You will be defined by the

actions you take every day.

206. Dreaming about what you want to be or what you want to achieve is good. You may even have planned the things you want to do...to be done or achieved in the long run. But, in order for you to achieve those dreams, you need to build a real, strong, stable foundation for your dreams to come true.

207. Just thinking about who you want to be must be coupled with the drive, determination, and passion to be the person you want to be.

208. A touch of imagination is needed if you are to succeed. Being imaginative can take you to great extremes.

209. You are in charge of your life. No one can force you to do things you don't want to do. So if you are aiming for something today, start immediately.

210. The winners came about through a continuous attempt to win. If you want to be considered a winner in life, you have to keep going even if you keep losing. Eventually you will reach the goal and become the winner.

211. They say that if you succeed, then you are happy. The truth is that success depends on happiness. Do what you love most and in time, you will reach the level of success you have always wanted.

212. Feel the need to be successful and eventually you will become one.

213. Remembering things is easier said than done, especially if you are living a busy life. But if you want to test your memory, then try to remember the things you did a year ago. Remember, every day is a journey worth living and remembering.

214. It takes a lot of strength and courage to speak softly and still be able to communicate effectively. Remember, you don't have to raise your voice if you want to make a comment.

Chapter 17: Living Life

215. Whatever happens, life must go on. There's nothing you can do to stop it. You just have to live it.

216. Life is not complicated, but it is we humans who make life difficult. Like, love, live simply and everything else will follow.

217. Trust that in time, you will be able to achieve what you want to have in life. Just make sure you act on your dreams and remain persistent. In the long run, you will be living the life you have always dreamed of.

218. When you say that living life to the fullest doesn't mean you only have to live for yourself. You also have to do things for others with an open heart if you want to say with certainty that you have lived a life of dignity.

219. The only constant thing in this world is change. Do not live in the past. You have to accept that things will always change if you wish to live fully now and be able to face the future head on.

220. Living life means accepting its challenges and understanding its lessons. This is the only way to fully understand the cycle of life.

221. The best things in life cannot be bought.

Man cannot live only with the material things he can afford. You need to give a part of yourself while living your life in order for it to be considered meaningful.

222. Being a happy and fortunate person will not help you reach your full potential. You need to take life seriously if you want to become someone.

223. There will always be times when you feel that you cannot handle the things that life has been giving you. Always remember that successful and happy people have to start somewhere and that they also have their own set of challenges. Just go ahead and do everything you can to overcome those challenges. In the end, you will find yourself at peace and happy with what you have achieved.

224. Some people have disabilities, but that doesn't stop them from appreciating and living life to the fullest. The only thing that can sustain and one that can be considered man's greatest disability is a bad attitude. If you lose it, you will have everything you have ever wanted.

225. Every living thing is worth everything when it still exists. If you have fully understood that every person, creature, and plant around you is worth living, then you are more likely to be on the road to preserving it than to destroying it.

226. Never give up in spite of all the qualities and failures you have experienced or are still experiencing at this time. You need to take

these things constructively and do your best to learn from them. This is the only way to become a better person.

227. They say that wealth controls everything. But if you think about it, you can have all the wealth in the world but still be unhappy. It is because love is the center of everything and if you understand and accept this fact wholeheartedly you can move forward freely and live life to the fullest.

Chapter 18: Unconditional Love

228. Love is not a mere emotion felt for a very special person. Love is a form of commitment that will endure no matter what.

229. There are several ways you can use to show that you love a person. You can say "I love you" a thousand times but it doesn't make sense if your action proves otherwise.

230. Love is the center of everything good in this life. Do not ignore love. It is what makes you a person and it is the only thing that will make you truly happy.

231. They say that your eyes allow you to see things. But the truth is that there are things you can only see and feel with your heart. Don't settle for just the things you can see. You also have to consider how your heart reacts to them.

232. In life, you will feel love and hate. For some, hate endures and outweighs love. It must be the other way around if you really want to get rid of all the emotional baggage you carry.

233. Your life will only have meaning if you know how to love.

234. Face each day with a smile. Face each person you meet with a smile. It is a simple gesture that can become something great like

love.

235. You will gain knowledge not only through education, but by living a life full of love.

236. A life accustomed to love is a life worth living.

237. In addition to experience, love is also a great teacher.

238. Trusting a person is the greatest proof that you love him.

239. One can never say that one lives life to the full if one does not know how to love.

Love is a great feeling which every person should enjoy because it is more omnipotent than wealth.

240. With faith you can make your dreams come true and with love you can do all things without complications and simply.

Chapter 19: Accepting Change

241. Accepting change is difficult at first and quite problematic in the middle. But once you have gone through the whole phase of accepting chance, which you will consider to be one of life's best experiences.

242. There are many things you may want to change in this world. The best thing you can do is to start with yourself.

243. Life will go on even with constant change.

244. Changing the world also means changing yourself for the better. This is a good start. Be as considerate of others as you can. Commit yourself to all the things you do. Begin the change within yourself.

245. People are always complaining about the bad things that happen in this world. If you want to contribute to change for the better, you must start with yourself and stop complaining.

246. The best way to change the world for the better is to become an educated person and use your knowledge to help others improve.

247. If you really want to change, you need to start with yourself, right now! You don't have to wait until tomorrow. You don't have to

wait for anyone else.

248. There are things that can change over time, but there are also things that only you can change.

249. Blaming others is a natural defense mechanism of man, especially if it is his fault. But if you really want to change for the better, you have to accept your faults and begin to change at that moment.

250. Don't be stubborn. There are things that will change even if you don't want to. You just have to change the way you see things, like the way these things change. That way, you can also adapt and change for the better.

251. If you don't know how to change your mind in situations, discussions, and simple things, then you can't expect to change and become a better human being.

252. You cannot change the world alone, but starting change with yourself can influence others to do the same and eventually lead to a better world.

253. If you have learned the true meaning of life then you must know by now how important change is.

254. Your life belongs to you and if you wish to live it fully then you must begin to accept the changes.

255. The words you say and write can affect many people and even the world. Use them well.

256. You may not notice it now, but every small change you make today can make a significant difference in what tomorrow will bring.

257. You can begin to change but by thinking good thoughts instead of bad ones.

Chapter 20: The Art of Letting Go

258. You cannot move forward if you do not know how to forgive.

259. If you want to be considered a strong person, you must learn that letting go is much better than clinging to your past.

260. Learn to let go of all the things that happened yesterday and only then will you appreciate the wonderful journey you will have today.

261. Saying goodbye is not always a bad

thing. There are times when it does more good for you and your life.

262. If you wish to overcome your weakness, you can begin by letting go and forgiving others.

263. God said to forgive your enemies. In addition to getting rid of the burden caused by hatred, your enemies will also be upset by your act of kindness and forgiveness.

264. Forgiveness is difficult to do, but when you do it, it can give you the relief and peace of mind you have always wanted.

265. You have no way of changing all that has happened in the past. But by forgiving,

you are sure to change everything that the future holds for you.

266. Man can be so forgiving and you may not even know it. However, he also needs to learn to forgive himself and only then can he move forward.

267. As a man, there will come a time when you will have to forgive those who have hurt you. Only then will you be able to live fully.

268. You can never feel loved if you yourself do not know how to forgive.

269. Forgiveness is an act that will warm your heart and relieve the pain you feel.

270. Forgiveness is an act of a person, but if you want to reunite with your enemy, you must both learn to forgive each other.

271. The greatest gift you can give to yourselves, which is beyond wealth, is to learn to forgive.

272. You can never hope to have a bright future if you are trapped in the past and cannot forgive others who have hurt you.

273. We all have to let go of our past and so do you.

274. You have a better chance of winning in the future if you can only forgive others and let go of your past.

275. Have the courage to stop living in the past and in doing so, you will have to have the strength to move forward and live the life you have always dreamed of.

Chapter 21: Family Issues

276. Feeling at home goes far beyond living in a house for several years. This feeling is triggered by the people you live with in your home.

277. Wealth is nothing compared to the love your family and friends can give you.

278. One important thing you should treasure in life is your family.

279. Having a family is like experiencing heaven on earth.

280. Business is important, but your family should always be your priority.

281. If you want to have a happy family, you must always be ready to be there for better or worse.

282. Value your family more than anything else because without them, it is like being in a cold, dark place.

283. Your money is not the only thing that should matter to you; you should treasure your connections with your friends and family.

284. Always remember that your family has always been there for you. They are your link

to your past, your strength in the present and your bridge to the future.

285. Nature has given us many things, and one of the most important things she has given you is your gift of family.

286. The basic unit of society is the family. Make sure you are proud to have one of your own.

287. If you have a family, you will never be forgotten or neglected.

Someone will always be there for you.

288. You may want many things in life, but you must realize that your family will always be there for you after every search.

289. Your family will give you strength to go on in life.

290. There is no other place where you can act terribly and still be loved, but your home.

291. You cannot choose your family, but you can choose to love them with all your heart.

292. Your home is not a mere structure; your home is the people who live there. Those same people who love you unconditionally. Cherish your family and never take them for granted.

Chapter 22: Courage and Strength are Vital

293. Be brave. You'll need it if you want to succeed in life.

294. Courage and strength are the key when it comes to living life to the fullest.

295. Anything that doesn't kill you will make you a stronger person.

296. There are several virtues and the most important one is courage.

297. Without the virtue of courage, you can never practice all the other virtues.

298. If you want to be considered a strong person, you must recognize the strength that others have.

299. Your will gives you strength and not your physique.

300. Fixing men who have been broken by the experiences they have had in life is difficult, but ensuring that your children grow strong and brave is something you can do easily.

301. Treat each day as a new opportunity to be stronger and braver.

302. Life will challenge you and as you go through each difficulty, you will become a better person.

303. You may feel broken by all the difficulties you have gone through, but you will become a much stronger person.

304. Keep holding on even if you think you no longer have the strength to go on.

305. Become a stronger person by living with dignity.

306. A strong person is an honorable person. In all the actions you do every day, you must make sure that there is honor in every one of

them.

307. By experiencing the pain of life, you become braver and stronger.

308. Eventually you will meet a person who will take you to your limits and to your state of weakness. Turn the situation around and use that perceived weakness as your source of strength.

309. Find the difference between being really strong and just feeling strong.

310. You will increase your strength as a person every time you overcome a difficulty.

311. Being fearless means knowing who you are and being strong means knowing others.

312. Do the things you once thought you could not do.

313. Gain the strength and courage you have always wanted by facing your fear head-on.

314. Inspire your ambition by being fearless.

315. Develop your strength through your life experiences.

316. Achieve success by going through various kinds of trials and suffering.

317. Belief in cause and effect can help you become a strong person.

318. Luck has nothing to do with success. You have to be strong and brave and have less faith in luck.

Chapter 23: Becoming a True Leader

319. Being a true leader means not only having the title, but also excellent service.

320. A true leader means giving hope through service.

321. If you wish to be a true leader, you must know how to find the best way, go through that chosen path and show the way to others.

322. Being a leader does not mean that you have to do everything possible to get all the credit.

323. Empower other people and you will be considered a true leader by your constituents.

324. Mold yourself to become a true leader by molding consensus and not just seeking it.

325. Get results and become a good leader because leadership goes beyond making speeches.

326. If you want to be distinguished as a leader and not a follower, you have to be innovative.

327. You do not position yourself as the god of others, but as a leader who can follow you on the path to greater good and success.

328. If you are productive, then expect your team to be productive as well.

329. If you want to be a leader, then you have to start thinking about solutions. But if you want to become a follower, then you can keep complaining about the problems.

330. If you are a mere follower, then you only need to manage yourself. But if you want to become a leader then you need to manage others using your heart.

331. Managing people means that you have to motivate them and help them reach their full potential.

332. Being a leader means making sure that

the ladder is the place for success.

333. You have to be efficient if you want you and your team to succeed.

334. Being responsible is important when it comes to being a good leader.

335. You must influence others to do things right and not order them to follow all your orders.

Chapter 24: Building Your Legacy

336. Use your brain when you face things and create a plan using your heart when you execute it.

337. You will surely leave a legacy if you live your life honestly.

338. Our names will be engraved on our own gravestone, but before that happens, it is always better to leave a mark on the hearts of those you meet.

339. When you leave, there is nothing you

can take with you. You can also leave this world knowing that you have left something good behind. Strive for that kind of legacy and you will leave this world a happy man.

340. What you do for others will remain your legacy once you are gone.

341. Strive for excellence, live with honor and love everyone you meet. For when the time comes for your life to end, your name will be sealed with a title worth remembering.

342. Do something that will remain even after your death.

343. Live your life and build a legacy that will leave an imprint on the hearts of those you

know and those you wish to help. This will leave an imprint that others will remember and even follow when you die.

344. Do not contribute to the violence that reigns in this world because one day, when you are gone, all that you leave behind will be a legacy that will only contribute to the existing chaos.

Chapter 25: Strive for Success

345. If you want to succeed, you need to develop habits that will help you do so.

346. The road to success is never easy, but if you really want to succeed, you must first deal with simple situations. Get as much experience and knowledge as possible and work your way through the most difficult tasks. In the end, you will be able to handle anything that comes your way.

347. Being successful means you need to have self-discipline. You should never let your state of mind get the better of you and you

should never allow yourself to simply go with the flow.

348. No matter how difficult things are right now, especially when you are trying to be the best you can be, never lose hope. You will get over it in time.

349. When you try to be the best and succeed in your endeavor, you will face obstacles. You can either destroy that obstacle or overcome it. In some cases, you may even be forced to find another way and avoid the obstacle you face altogether. No matter what you choose, you will know in your heart what the best thing you can do is.

350. Think positive even if you face many difficulties.

351. Hope will help you to get ahead and give you strength to pursue your dreams.

352. In addition to thinking positively, your actions should also be positive.

353. Anyone can succeed. You just have to focus on achieving your goals.

354. Successful individuals spend their time wisely, and if you want to be like them, then you should do so.

355. Be open-minded and calm, especially when faced with difficulties. This will help you make the right decisions.

356. Increase your chances of success by checking out different viewpoints, gathering new ideas, focusing on your goals and checking out new opportunities to help you achieve the success you have always wanted.

357. Don't make excuses. This is only for people who are either lazy or too scared. If you want to succeed, you have to act on it.

358. Success doesn't just depend on doing things for your own benefit. In many cases, you have a better chance of becoming one if you do it for others as well.

359. Without hard work, you can never hope to become a successful person.

360. Make sure you are always in good physical shape. This will help you as it will be the source of your energy. Without it, you can't do all the things you want to do and if you ever try, you may not get it right.

361. Live a life with a principle and do things to achieve success according to a set of constructive principles.

362. You do things for a reason. Therefore, begin your quest for success with good reason in mind.

363. Never give up. You can only succeed if your determination is unwavering.

364. You need to master your craft if you want to succeed.

365. When you read quotes and motivational advice, you must make sure you read between the lines and find the wisdom you are looking for.

Here we end this wonderful journey of motivation. I hope this book has released the potential you have within you!

SUCCESS AND PROSPERITY!

THE ABILITY TO SOLVE PROBLEMS

BOOK 2

THE ABILITY TO SOLVE PROBLEMS

Introduction

You probably use problem solving every day. It's often taken for granted. People don't realize how wonderful and important problem solving is. Most people don't even recognize it as a skill. In fact, most of the time, problem solving comes naturally.

Problem solving can be defined as an art. The art of problem solving is something we learn at a very early age. It helps us throughout our lives and is something we could not live without. Being able to solve problems is a life skill. It is important and must be taken seriously to get the best results.

Seeing problem solving as an art can help you appreciate it more.

You can start using problem solving to its fullest potential and really respect that problem solving is important. You just need to learn more about problem solving as a skill and an art.

Chapter 1: The Importance of Problem Solving

Problem solving is a fixed element in life. You have to be able to solve problems. Problems arise every day. Sometimes they are small and sometimes they are big. Sometimes the solution to a problem is a matter of life and death and other times it is simply a matter of keeping your sanity. Regardless of why you need to solve a problem, you cannot deny that you need it.

If you are a parent, then problem solving is a skill you certainly couldn't live without.

Children are full of problems, and as a parent it's up to you to help them find the solution. Sometimes you have to be creative because problems that arise can be quite difficult to solve without a little creative thinking.

The same can be said in business. Companies have a lot of problems and it's up to the employees to find the way to solve them. Again, sometimes simple problem-solving techniques don't work because some problems require more skills to solve.

You encounter problems every day, from flat tires to saving a failing product line. You are a problem solver and probably don't even realize it. However, you should pay attention to your problem-solving skills.

It is common for people to take problem solving for granted. We do it so much that it's not hard to believe that it comes naturally. It is this familiarity with problem solving that leads us to take it for granted and to no longer be creative in problem solving.

If you think about how you solved problems when you were a child, you were probably much more creative then. Now you probably go straight to the tried and true methods instead of trying new things.

The problem with this, however, is that taking problem solving for granted can make you a lazy problem solver. You may no longer waste time trying to solve a problem, but go for a tried and true solution. It may not be the best solution, but because you are a wise problem solver, you don't take the time to use your problem-solving skills to try to find a better solution.

Problem solving can be an amazing process, but it's up to you to make it happen rather than something you do because you have to. You have the ability to become a great problem solver, but you have to start looking at it as an art.

Chapter 2: Problem solving from a child's point of view

As mentioned, children solve problems very differently from adults. This is because children have less problem-solving ability and much less experience in problem solving. However, the way children solve problems can teach a lot.

A child approaches a problem with an open mind. It's probably not something you do. You probably approach a problem with some preconceived notions about how it will all end. You probably approach it with a negative attitude and see the problem as a nuisance. A child, on the other hand, sees it as a challenge. They think a problem is a big mystery and are excited about solving it.

They're likely to get frustrated when they can't solve the problem right away. A child, however, will get more excited. They will try different things until they find what works.

They will experiment and continue to do so until they succeed.

A child solves problems with wonder, amazement and persistence. Adults want problems to solve themselves because they want to take the time to solve them correctly.

The difference between the way adults and

children solve problems says a lot about how much we take problem solving for granted. Adults tend to be so concerned about how long it takes to solve a problem that they are actually happy to succeed in solving a problem.

If you can simply hint at child-like problem solving techniques, you'll find that problem solving becomes easier and more enjoyable. You will begin to see problem solving as an art and not an inconvenience. You will be incorporating **SKILLS**.

Chapter 3: Aspects of Problem Solving

The art of problem solving involves more than just jumping to the easiest solution. You have to take the time to analyze the problem. You have to come up with several solutions so that you can find the perfect one. You have to make a conscious effort to solve a problem in a new way or the best way.

Here are some aspects of problem solving that you should start using. You should take these aspects and apply them the next time you have a problem, no matter how big or small. Then you will be able to understand the art of problem solving.

- **Be flexible:** As mentioned, you have to go beyond your comfort zone. You have to avoid the immediate urge to go for the tried and true. You have to be flexible and willing to try something different. You will never know how big a solution can be if you don't try it.

- **Take time to think:** You may have to step back and consider the situation before you act. You should brainstorm a little about the different ways you can solve this problem. Discuss your options and stop before you act.

- **Ask questions:** Part of solving a problem is creating new questions to answer. You may think this is silly and makes the problem worse, but actually asking questions will lead to deeper solutions.

- **Look at the problem in a different way:** Don't approach the problem as you normally would. Try to think differently. Avoid your natural tendencies. This can be difficult at first, but once you get used to thinking differently, it will become natural.

- **Think unconventionally:** Think of solutions that don't make sense. You may be surprised to find an unconventional idea that is the perfect solution to your problem.

Using these ideas you can start to look at problem solving in a whole new way. Not only will you jump to the obvious conclusion, but you will be able to actually find the perfect solution.

All it really involves is taking a step back and taking some time. Not all problems need to be solved immediately. It is those problems that really allow you to put the art of problem solving to good use.

Chapter 4: Problem-Solving Skills

Problem solving involves many different skills. The most important skills are described below.

- **Creative thinking:** You have to be able to think creatively and see beyond the obvious if you want to be a good problem solver. You can't limit yourself to the obvious because in most cases that will never solve the problem. You have to be willing to think differently, brainstorm and come up with a unique solution. Creative thinking can make a person a perfect problem solver. Being able to think creatively allows a person to come up with solutions to problems that others don't even think about. A person is able to come up with good ideas that may not be so obvious. Creative thinking is something that can be a great benefit to almost any profession because quick thinking is a great skill.

- **Reasoning:** Reasoning has a place in problem solving, but it is important not to let your reasoning outweigh your creativity. Reasoning is very useful, because it will help you eliminate the good ideas from the bad ones in order to arrive at the final solution.

- **Objectivity:** You have to be objective when you approach a problem. You can't have preconceived notions about how the situation will end or how you can fix the problem quickly. You have to approach a problem with an open mind and the ability to try different things to solve it.

- **Positive attitude:** Your attitude can contribute greatly to your success as a problem solver. You need to be positive. If you approach a problem thinking you won't be able to solve it, then you probably won't be able to. You have to think positive and believe in yourself.

These skills will help you to be a good problem solver. The above skills are some of the main things you need to be able to solve problems in a constructive way.

If you have these skills then you need to

refine them. If you do not have these skills then you need to work on them. If you are committed to becoming a good problem solver then you need to have these skills to help you.

You can build on these skills to help you be a better problem solver as well.

There are also other skills not listed above that can help you be a good problem solver.

You just need to identify what things you already know or can do that might be useful in solving problems.

Make a list of your skills. You will find that many things you may not see exactly as a skill are actually a very good asset to your problem-solving skills. Review your skills and see how each one can benefit your problem-solving ability in some way.

Chapter 5: Finding a Problem-Solving Method

Not everyone will solve problems in the same way. That's only part of what makes us each unique individuals. However, you can learn from others and how they solve problems. You can use a technique that is new to you or something that really works and you would like to use. Watch how others solve problems and see what you can learn from them.

There are many methods of problem solving. You probably use one method and stick to it to solve every problem you encounter. This can be a bad thing. You should try different methods because sometimes one method works better for a particular problem than another.

There are three main ways to solve problems:

1. Questions: Some people solve problems by asking questions. They look at the problem and ask "What if" - what if I try this or what if this happens? Through the questions they are able to see the possible results. This allows them to find the best solution that seems to work to solve the problem.

2. Develop a process: For the more organized individual or the more complex problem it can sometimes help to develop a problem-solving process. This usually involves analyzing the problem, proposing different solutions, testing the solutions and finally applying the chosen solution. It is a very structured way of solving a problem.

3. Brainstorming: For the most creative problem solvers, there is the brainstorming process. This involves simply sitting down and thinking of numerous ways to solve the problem. Some ideas may be out there and that's okay. Using innovative thinking and being creative can help a person find an unconventional solution to a problem.

Being able to solve problems is a natural thing that we are all born with. It is really how you approach problem solving that will help determine how good you are at solving them.

You should be willing to try different methods and different ways of solving problems. This will allow you to be able to propose many options as solutions to your problem.

This will give you a better chance of finding the perfect solution and putting the art of problem solving into practice

Once you have developed a good understanding of problem solving that goes beyond the basic need for it, you can then begin to recognize and truly understand the idea of problem solving as an art.

You are able to start using problem solving in a different way. You can begin to become a master of problem solving. People will begin to see you as the person of solution. They will come to you for advice and help when they have problems.

You will also be able to avoid problems in your life and solve them when they arise. You will soon discover that the art of problem solving is something you cannot live without.

Being able to see problem solving in a different way will help you approach problems differently. You will not be afraid of them when they appear, but will embrace them and begin to work on finding a solution.

In addition to dealing with problems, problem solving will help you to make your life much more fluid. You will be able to handle adversity more easily. In the long run, you will begin to feel better about yourself and be happier in general.

Problem solving is not just a skill, but an art. It can change your life for the better. Being able to solve problems quickly and efficiently is something that not everyone can do.

Not everyone can see a problem and take it as a challenge. Some people just fall apart in the face of problems. These people have a hard time in life and in business. They can get to the top of the game with their problem-solving skills.

It all starts with the ability to recognize problems and put problem-solving methods to good use. You have to stay calm and level-headed so you can look for the solution that works best.

Chapter 6: Renouncing the Negative

One of the keys to becoming a good problem solver is to give up the negative. You have to approach problem solving in a positive way or you will never get anywhere.

Many times people approach a problem with the already formed mind that they will never solve it. If you think you can't do something, then you are likely to fail when you try. You have to think positively. You have to face a problem thinking I can solve it, there is no problem.

A positive attitude is to keep an open mind, which is important for problem solving in general. When you approach a problem with a positive attitude, you can easily avoid getting frustrated. You're more open to letting your ideas flow, and you're more likely to try various solutions.

A positive attitude may be the only one you have. Think about how you approach problems. Do you always get into the situation thinking you will never solve the problem? If so, then maybe simply changing your attitude can improve your problem-solving ability.

Give it a try. Next time you approach a problem, think positively. Tell yourself that you can do it, that you can solve the problem. Don't get carried away with the negative.

A positive attitude is an important thing when it comes to solving problems. Don't forget that your attitude can be a big influence. Keep it positive to get the best results.

Chapter 7: Problem Solving Exercises

There are many ways to practice problem solving. You just have to take the time to practice. As with any skill, the more you work on it, the better you will do. You have to practice to be a good problem solver.

Here are some exercises you can do to help you be a better problem solver, open your mind and get into the problem-solving state of mind.

Exercise 1: Play games. Any kind of game, whether it is a board game, a card game, or even a word search, will open your mind. It makes you think. It helps you solve problems and put your mind into problem-solving mode. Play often so you can develop your mind and get used to solving problems.

Exercise 2: Play with a child Children are free to think. They use their imagination all the time. They see the world around them as amazing and exciting. They are constantly exploring. They love to tackle problems. Spending some time with a child will allow you to see the world the way they do. You can take away some of their wonder and amazement that you can use in your problem solving.

Exercise 3: Experiencing something new when you try something new you are gaining new things, expanding your mind and opening yourself up to new problems that need to be solved. You will be able to practice your problem solving and learn something at the same time.

Exercise 4: Solving problems that already have a solution Practice makes perfect, so you need to practice solving problems. The best way to do this is to take on problems that have already been solved. Find out how the solution was found.

How was the solution found? By examining the solution to a problem you can learn a lot about the process of problem solving. You can get some key information from this exercise that will help you solve problems in the future.

These four exercises aren't the only things you can do, but you should have a pretty good idea of what you need to do to help you start thinking like a master at solving problems. It's all about opening your mind and practicing your problem-solving methods.

Chapter 8: An Example of Problem Solving at Work

The concept of how children solve problems versus how adults solve problems must be fully understood. It is very important because we lose those good problem-solving skills as we grow up.

Part of the reason for this is that we become more logical. We don't want to try to be creative anymore. We want to go straight to what we're sure will work. We don't try anything else and if what we think will work doesn't work, we get frustrated.

Another thing is that we lose our sense of experimentation. We don't want to take the time to try out different ideas or even come up with different ideas. We get lazy.

As already mentioned, children do things very differently. Here is an illustrated example of how a child and an adult would approach the same problem.

Situation: Matias and his son, Matias junior, are given a video game system to connect to a TV. Matias is 28 years old and Junior 8. Neither has instructions and neither has set up a system like this before.

Matias: Matias' first instinct is to take out all the cables and parts and place them properly. Then he examines each piece to see how everything fits together. He determines that there should be a cable that goes from the TV to the game system and takes one that looks good. Then hook all the wires to the points where they seem to go and turn the system on just to find out that nothing is wrong. Unhook everything and try again and again. Eventually he gets frustrated and asks if the system is broken.

Junior: Junior dives right into the connecting cords. He ends up with the system connected to the TV, but nothing happens. He realizes he forgot to hook up the system and does it, but that doesn't make him show up on the TV. Instead of unhooking everything, he starts playing with the TV. He finishes changing the channel and violates the system that's working.

Matias quickly gives up and forgets the obvious: turn the system on. Matias' first instinct was to give an excuse and say that the system was broken. Junior kept trying and trying new things until he found out.

The difference in how they solved the problem is clear. Matias probably would have solved it eventually, but Junior was the one who really succeeded. He never gave up and was willing to experiment. He also didn't miss the obvious because he was as focused on other things as his father.

The way kids solve problems is amazing. It's really something you can learn from.

When you solve a problem, strive to be more like Junior and less like Matias.

Conclusion

Problem solving is an art because it takes a true creative mind to be a good problem solver. It involves creative thinking and is something you can learn to do. As an art, it should be held in high esteem. Problem solving should be taken seriously, but not too seriously.

As has been shown, adults tend to lose their problem-solving skills. Adults are too quick to want to do things. They don't take the time to really think. Thinking is an important part of problem solving. Thinking involves not only looking at the obvious but also considering the not-so-obvious.

Children are masters of problem solving because they are not afraid to try anything.

Children will work and experiment and take time to solve a problem. They don't care if people think they are weird for taking so much time to solve a problem. They have fun trying to solve problems and see it as a challenge or a game rather than a job.

Adults, on the other hand, prefer to give up rather than make an effort. They see problem solving as one more thing they have to do. It's the job. There's nothing fun about it.

They can't see that problem solving can be something fun and exciting - it's just the way you approach it and look at it. That's why we have to rethink problems and approach them the same way we did when we were kids.

We need to approach problems with a positive attitude. You have to believe that you can solve the problem and not immediately think about how difficult it is going to be. You have to believe in your abilities. Doubt can kill even the best efforts to solve the problem.

If you never believe you can solve a problem, then you will probably never be able to solve it.

Your mind is very powerful. You've probably been told before that anything you put into your mind can be accomplished. Well, the same is true for what your mind is against. If you think you can't do something, then you won't be able to do it. It's really that simple. Your mind is that powerful. Mind over matter, that saying says it all.

You have to try different things and work towards a solution instead of waiting for the solution to become clear. You have to work at solving problems, but at the same time you have to be creative in solving problems.

Problem solving is something we were born to do. Problems come in all shapes and sizes. They can be small or they can be huge. You must always be prepared because most of the time problems come unexpectedly. They'll just show up and you'll have to deal with them.

You can't avoid problems, so it makes sense to be a good problem solver. A good problem solver is going to be an asset. He's someone good to have around.

Become that problem solver. Be the person everyone loves to have around. Be the person who can look at a complex situation and find a solution. Don't be the person who runs away and says I don't know or I can't do it.

There is no room for negative words when it comes to solving problems. Always remember that. Remember Matias and Junior too. Be a junior, not a Matias. Don't give up or make excuses. Face the problems and make an effort to solve them. Put your mind to it and you can be a great problem solver.

Put the art of problem solving to work in your life and you will be surprised how well it works. Stop giving up and passing them on to others. Solve your problems and you'll be glad you did.